Rot and Not

A collection of poems
(nonsensical and otherwise)
by John Dean
with illustrations by Erik Sansom.

HB
HARVEY BOOKS

Rot and Not © 2008 John Dean.
johnmichaeldean@yahoo.co.uk

Published by Harvey Books.
First Edition 2008.

Illustrations by Erik Sansom
esansom@sympatico.ca

Typesetting and repro by Book Printers Limited.
Printed in Great Britain on FSC paper.
www.bookprinters.co.uk

ISBN 978 0 946988 84 6

For Lady M

By the same author

Desideratum Enigmatum	1978	Outposts Publications
Stuff and Nonsense	2006	Harvey Books
I Wish...	2007	Harvey Books
I Wish... Some More	2007	Harvey Books

Acknowledgements

Assistance in editing was provided by Victoria Smith, Lucy Dean and Kevin Inskip.

Knots by R D Laing was the inspiration behind *I Think*.

The book *Eats, Shites and Leaves* by Antal Parody proved to be a useful source of ideas, resulting in *Great Mysteries, I Interject!* and *A Sewer can fall down a Sewer*.

The title *Vacant Seas* was taken from a line of a poem by Pauline Hawkesworth.

Parting was inspired by *The Life Beyond* by Rupert Brooke.

In the Land with not a Flower is an adaptation of *O'er Seas That Have No Beaches* by Mervyn Peake.

The Problem with Bananas is a parody of *The Trouble with Geraniums* by Mervyn Peake

A *Fred* illustration by Rupert Fawcett provided the inspiration for *My Cereal Collection*.

In the three verses of *All Nonsense* the first lines are lines of poems by Mervyn Peake, Lewis Carroll and Edward Lear respectively.

Sir John Betjeman wrote *All Electric down from London* and this inspired the *All Infected* version.

William Roe suggested that there should be a poem about the author on the back cover.

Contents

Introduction

Having written several books of poems for children I decided it was time to compile an adult collection. I use the word "nonsense" to describe much of my work, but the term is not entirely accurate since there is usually something meaningful to be found within. I just like to set things in a nonsensical form.

My first thought was to put together a humorous collection. The majority of my poems fit into this category, but then I decided to display all aspects of my work. So I will take the reader on something of an emotional roller-coaster ride. Usually I will be up there with the pun and the quip and the *double entendre,* but occasionally I plummet into the depths of despair with a poem about lost love or the terrors of an existential reality. Sometimes I will even attempt the two extremes in the same poem, with comedy in tragedy and tragedy in comedy.

In my mid-twenties I gained an interest in Eastern philosophy. It contains elements that fit very well into a nonsensical outlook, and so it affected my work then and has influenced me ever since.

With my poems for children I gained inspiration from the works of Lewis Carroll and Edward Lear. In this collection there is the added influence of Mervyn Peake and Rupert Brooke. I came across the adult nonsense of Mervyn Peake in the early Seventies. His style suited me perfectly and without his influence my work would never have developed as it did. My love poems owe much to the Romantic poets of the Nineteenth Century, but it was the love poems of Rupert Brooke that really made a mark on me.

A habit of collecting jokes has also affected my work. I like to convert them into poems, so some of the ideas behind my shorter works may be familiar to you.

My general style is brief and to the point. Very few of my poems are more than four verses long, and I might be a little old-fashioned, but I do like a poem to rhyme and to have metre. However, I venture into a more modern approach on occasions. I do not go along with those who claim that every word in a poem has to be the right one. Sometimes I will use a word simply because I like the sound it makes. A poem can be like a piece of music, but a composer is never expected to explain the significance of every note.

My poems are a direct reflection of my personality, but I make no apologies for that. I do what I must do, and so I express myself warts and all. Poetry may not appeal to the majority, but if it is raw and unpretentious then it stands a better chance of doing so. At least I remain jolly for the most part. In addition I must point out that much of my poetry is written in colloquial English, so those who cannot tolerate the informality of grammatical imperfections are advised to read elsewhere.

There may be something in the claim that boys never grow up, so let me apologise for the toilet humour in advance.

Morning Sickness is my bid to claim the shortest poem. There is a three-word poem entitled *Fleas,* and without quoting it word for word it considers the idea that Adam must have possessed them. But my two-word poem about Eve just pips it.

When I wrote *On a Special Species* I had no intention of making it into the shape of a cat, but once it was on the computer I accidentally pressed the centre alignment button and there it was. All I needed to do to complete the job was to turn the first line into ears, to turn the perfectly placed O's into eyes and to add the whiskers and tail. Even the collar was in place from the outset. So it was just another of those weird events that happens in life.

Talking to Women has been written in a *Ghazal*-like style, the *Ghazal* being a form of traditional Arabian verse. The word *Ghazal* literally means *Talking to Women.*

I wish to express my thanks to my Canadian illustrator, Erik Sansom. He serves me so well in bringing my poems to life. Having someone from the other side of the pond adds a special flavour to my work. Things might have been dull and British without him, but with his input something quirky and mid-Atlantic has resulted.

I eventually decided to include location and date for each poem, thinking that it might enhance appreciation. I started writing poems in the early Seventies, but many of the poems in this collection have been written during the last few years. A major lull is evident during the Eighties and Nineties, but this was the time that I was busily engaged in the art of raising my daughter.

I must make it clear that I do not consider myself to be a poet. I am just someone who plays around with words and ideas. If I can make the reader think and/or laugh then my work is done.

Further copies of this book and copies of my books for children can be obtained from the website and e-mail addresses below.

John Dean

johnmichaeldean.com

johnmichaeldean@btinternet.com

johnmichaeldean@yahoo.co.uk

I'm in the Ostrich Club

I'm in the Ostrich Club;
We meet up twice a week;
I run about and flap my arms
And wear a plastic beak.

The world around is struggling –
Should I give it a hand?
No, not when I can bury
My head here in the sand.

Portsmouth, 7 June 2006

I Think

I think she thinks I think too much
About her thoughts for me –
I think she might be right.

I think she thinks she's afraid to think
I think she thinks of fear
And I think she thinks my thoughts on this
Will one day disappear –
I think I'd better think again.

I think she thinks I think she thinks
I thought she thought she knew
That the fears she thought I feared for her
Were thoughtless and untrue –
And I think she thinks I think she thinks
I think she thinks so too –
I think.

Gosport, 17 April 1976

The Computer wasn't Working

The computer wasn't working
And I dialled the helpdesk number,
Then faded into bankruptcy,
Despair and senile slumber.

Eventually some youth answered,
But compounded my remorse –
He said, "Have you integrated
Your power supply at source?"

Portsmouth, 21 October 2006

Hark the Feral Budgies Sing!

Hark the feral budgies sing! –
They're out there in the yard! –
My budgies all escaped last week! –
Life can be so hard!

I'm sure that they are mocking me
All perched there on the wall.
"Who's a pretty boy, then?" –
Last night I heard one call.

In car, 9 March 2007

Flaunting with the Flautist

Sitting in the orchestra
Blowing on her flute –
Nowhere else within the Universe
Could someone be so cute.

Hoping she will notice me
Working my trombone,
As fed up as I can be
Living life alone.

Her golden hair flowing
With the energy she produces,
The way she smiles through every bar
And the pleasure it induces.

Clever little twirly bits
Of music coming out –
Were that me and not the flute
I'd faint from fun, no doubt.

Portsmouth, 29 September 2006

Twiddling

Living life is a crime,
Regret forever lingers –
Of late I seem to spend my time
Twiddling my fingers.

Imperfections have I many –
I can do my sums –
Embezzling every penny
Whilst twiddling my thumbs.

The innocent are still and stay,
The guilty person fidgets –
And so I pace around all day
Twiddling my digits.

Portsmouth, 4 October 2007

What Love is This?

What love is this
Save from our arms depart?
As is and was, in retrospect
Must we now disinfect
The notions of our play?
All living things have sinned –
Let's state it not amiss –
And be it known all ventures made
Will at some time come to this.

Birmingham, 11 March 1976

The Fable of Freddie Mottles

We all hide,
We hurt inside,
But we cover up the sin;
Freddie Mottles
Had his bottles
Of whisky, rum and gin.

When newly born
We rant and yawn
And create a colossal din;
Freddie Mottles
Had his bottles
Of whisky, rum and gin.

I'll eat anywhere,
I don't care,
And even from a tin;
Freddie Mottles
Had his bottles
Of whisky, rum and gin.

When I was a boy
Without a toy
I'd sit and suck my thumb;
Freddie Mottles
Had his bottles
Of whisky, gin and rum.

I work away
Through every day,
Go on through thick and thin;
Freddie Mottles
Had his bottles
Of whisky, rum and gin.

I try to smile
All the while,
But often end up glum;
Freddie Mottles
Had his bottles
Of whisky, gin and rum.

We have our games,
Our personal aims,
Our little wars to win;
Freddie Mottles
Had his bottles
Of whisky, rum and gin.

I like to see
My lover's knee,
It makes me feel quite frisky;
Freddie Mottles
Had his bottles
Of gin and rum and whisky.

My accountant's wife
Used a knife
Upon deciding to do herself in;
Freddie Mottles
Had his bottles
Of whisky, rum and gin.

My fable told,
Though sad and old,
Will sometimes win a grin;
Freddie Mottles
Had his bottles
Of whisky, rum and gin.

Gosport, 17 September 1975

Morning Sickness

Eve 'eaved.

Portsmouth, 26 July 2005

May I have Your Permission to Scream?

May I have your permission to scream?
It's happening – it isn't a dream!
Something crawling there under the duvet –
Such a malevolent menacing move, eh?

How dare such a creature intrude
When we're sleeping in here in the nude?
It has just put one leg on my thigh –
Any second I think I might die!

Portsmouth, 25 August 2006

I'm Standing in a Rut

I'm standing in a rut,
My eyes are at ground level,
In the family of ments
I have reached dishevel.

The game has turned against me,
Life has played its fatal card –
Your unexpected exit
Has hit me rather hard.

In car, 29 November 2006

Separation

How sadly goes the squalor of the day –
How quickly the joys, how slowly the tears –
And the crowds of conversation with nothing left to say
Are all that's left to bridge the passing years.

In the back streets every second is another surge of pain,
A sordid move beyond my empty room –
And I sit knowing that I must think of love again,
Staring in upon my filth and gloom.

Bombay (Mumbai), 18 September 1979

Soaps

I always have the soaps on,
It seems the thing to do –
There's five TV's in our house –
We've got one in the loo –

There's a new one in the kitchen
And I watch soaps from my bed,
And all the plots and counter-plots
Are there inside my head –

Romance, violence, accidents,
Sex and crime abound –
Time and time and time again,
The wheels go round and round.

But something isn't working!
What have I done wrong?
How can I experience life
When I watch it all day long?

Portsmouth, 23 March 1993

Great Mysteries

Why does my doctor own a practice? –
You'd think she'd get it right.
Why isn't phonetic spelled the way it sounds? –
How do you get off a non-stop flight?

Why is dyslexic such a complex word
For a problem linked with reading? –
I sit and pose these questions
And some answers I am needing.

And if no man is an island
Where does that leave the Isle of Man? –
Perhaps you can explain these things –
For I'm b******d if I can.

Portsmouth, 19 August 2007

Donations of Unrequited Love

Through the streets at midnight,
Alone now with the pain,
The rushing of the water
Gushing down the drain.

Umbrellas like propellers
Spinning all around –
Rain cascading, bouncing, fading,
Falling to the ground.

"What more than this is misery?" –
I feel the need to say –
So here a tear and there a tear
To help it on its way.

Birmingham, 8 December 1976

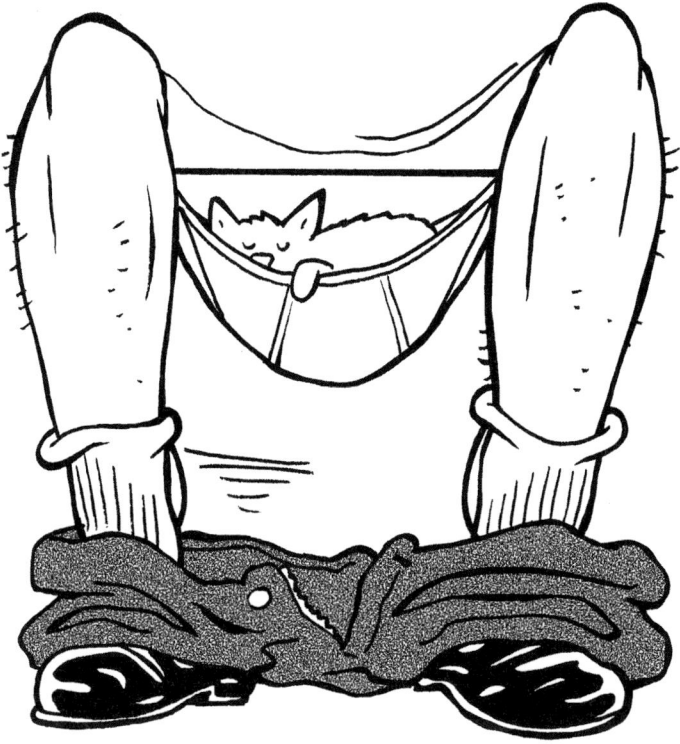

When I'm Sitting on the Toilet

When I'm sitting on the toilet,
My pants between my knees,
My kitten sits inside them –
Along with all his fleas.

It's like a cradle to him,
An open invitation –
And he finds the time to go asleep
When I have constipation.

Brighton, 26 November 2006

Initiation

The hour is upon me.
The footsteps of the millions
Trudging from the past
Echo on the avenue
And emphasise my fate.

Decision time.
No longer like the worm,
In my turning there is hope.
My hands are cold,
My prospects could be colder.
The shining street,
Soaked in fearful rain,
Reflecting back my lack of confidence
And my desperate need for pride.

Your door before me,
Your beauty shines within.
One knock and I must ask,
One knock and fate takes over.
Cometh the hour, cometh the man.

Portsmouth, 4 April 2007

Bad Boy

I've got myself three girlfriends,
I smother them with kisses –
The Sun shines on the righteous,
But occasionally it misses.

Havant, 8 August 2007

The Unforeseen Fly

The unforeseen fly was swift to descend –
I was having a meal with my wife and a friend.
With supply so a-plenty it wanted a share –
This delicate thing, as light as the air.
It was born in the filth where it munched out its youth,
And became as an adult profoundly uncouth –
From carcass to caviar, from faeces to feast –
This disgusting creature, this unwholesome beast.
To digest our food it dissolves it in sick,
But before it could do so I gave it a flick.
God made the Earth and the Moon and the sky –
But where was good taste when He thought of the fly?

Portsmouth, 3 April 2005

If Graduates were Commonplace

If graduates were commonplace
What a better world there'd be –
People with intelligence
To wait on you and me –

An announcer with good diction
To update us on the trains
And a squad of super scientists
To come and clear our drains.

Brighton, 22 July 2006

New York/New York

Back again.
Over thirty years have passed.

Loving confined spaces
I have missed your shadowed ways –
Your streets and avenues interlocking,
Some as tall as they are long.

Still your towers loom,
But two then had newly risen from the dust –
I stood between them and gazed upon their heights.

Then the terror,
Then the horror,
And the fall back to the dust.

There is a greater purpose –
In God we still trust.

New York, New York, 13 September 2007

Resentment

My wife is a good driver –
She says it's intuition –
And her hands never deviate
From the ten to two position –
That she will scrape the car one day
Is what I'm always wishin'.

Basingstoke, 29 November 2006

Alien Salvation

Europa is a cold home,
But in the waters far beneath
I can watch the oval creatures
On the frozen jagged reef
And the thoughts that they can offer me
Can bring such great relief.

The heavy Earth has gone now,
A distant memory –
Within the pull of Jupiter
My soul is whole and free –
The oval ones are helping
And they do so much for me.

In car, 9 November 2006

If with a Double But

If with a double but,
Perhaps with a single so –
Forgiving your destruction
Forgives me all I know.

I saw our world emerging,
Watched my love upon,
Waited till it vanished
And bellowed, "God, it's gone!"

I wander in the back streets,
I walk the gaudy stage,
Mimicking this fundamental
Self-indulgent age.

Birmingham, 9 February 1977

A Love Apart

Love means sharing everything,
Means offering the heart,
And yet my gentle love and I
Live many miles apart.

I see my love infrequently,
When I can make the journey there –
To hold her tightly to me,
To touch her flowing hair.

But love is all-pervading,
And from that moment then
I find the world has meaning
Until we meet again.

On train, 30 April 2004

No Milk Please

Delivering milk to
Our homes every day,
But why does he have
To get in the way? –

Blocking the road,
And he moves like a snail –
And when I'm late for work
He's there without fail.

But when I come down in the morning
He still hasn't been,
And a black tea or coffee
Is grossly obscene.

It might be unfair,
Unjust and naïve,
But I reckon he waits
Till his customers leave –

Then milk tends to go off
When it's left out all day
And in my neighbourhood
People steal it away.

What I hate most of all
Is when he comes for his money
And I'm having sex or a meal –
It just isn't funny.

As for the pint,
It's a thing of the past –
Three litres from Tescos –
That really does last.

Yes, there are traditions
That we ought to keep,
But if we lose the milkman
It's with joy that I'd weep.

Farnborough, 3 May 2006

Let Me Remark on You

Let me remark on you:
On the way your spirit
Seems to glow about her form,
On the joy within your footsteps
As you journey to and fro,
On the agitation of the heart
Through the flowing of your hair,
On the epicentre of perfection
Residing in your smile.

In a world of chaos
There is order,
There is peace;
In a world of disappointment
The fulfilment of a dream.

Let me remark on you –
The remarkable
And my love.

Portsmouth, 15 January 2008

Abra – Cadaver!

I'm a magpie through and through,
I live beside the road,
I do what magpies do
And I hate the Highway Code.

For fauna life is tragic –
A car brakes and shuffles gears –
And then, as if by magic,
Another meal appears.

In car, 16 October 2007

I Interject!

All I ever got from him:
Ahem! Good heavens! Hey!
Dear dear! Ho hum! Uh-hu!
Well well! Tut-tut! I say! –

Aha! My gosh! Heigh-ho!
Ooh! Oops! Ouch! Ow! Phooey!
But now at last he's gone away –
Hurrah! Ha-ha! Yippee!

Portsmouth, 2 December 2006

Vacant Seas

The seaside resorts of England
All creaking now with pain –
The people have deserted them
For the sunny climes of Spain.

In car, 18 October 2007

Late October, 8pm

A combination
Most obscene:
Teenagers and
Halloween.

I have something
Nice and neat:
Put an end to
Trick or Treat.

Portsmouth, 28 October 2006

On an Organelle

How fond we are
Of mitochondria –
Inside of us they live –
They work away
By night and day,
Pure energy to give –

These little pals
Within our cells –
And furthermore, it must be said,
That without their work –
Which they never shirk –
We would all be dead.

Portsmouth, 31 January 2006

Echoes in the Valley

Echoes in the valley
Recalling your demise,
Reflections in the silent stream
Of your departing eyes,
Memories of the paradise
Engulfed within your sighs.

Death did not deserve you,
You were so akin to life,
Lying on the slab now
Beneath the butcher's knife –
Sitting on the village green
Without my loving wife.

In car, 1 November 2006

My Name is Jake O'Donnell

My name is Jake O'Donnell,
I come from County Clare,
All my teeth have fallen out,
I'm losing all my hair –

A toe dropped off from frostbite
When I was twenty-three –
As the years go sailing by
There's less and less of me.

Portsmouth, 19 August 2006

An Impatient Young Fellow from Gloucester

An impatient young fellow from Gloucester
Upset his partner one day and he lost her –
He did feel remorse,
But that was mainly because
It was over a cliff and he tossed her.

Brussels, 30 April 2004

A Rose was a Rose was a Rose

Two minuses made a plus,
Or so it was with us –
As beneath the heavy earth
A miracle gave birth.

And so we grew, entwined our way
From the dark into the day,
Came up in essence as of one,
Blossomed out beneath the Sun.

What was ours was certain then,
It could not change – Oh no! not when
Such joy there was to be
Through you, the earth and me.

But roses now have other names
And there are other claims
Upon my lost and lonely soul –
One half of which was whole.

New Delhi, 7 October 1979

Imagine Behaving like Cattle

Imagine behaving like cattle:
Swallowing food as we do,
But then bringing it up again
And giving it another good chew.

It is hard to accept that they
Can gain satisfaction from it,
Slowly munching away at
Cold and clinging vomit.

Portsmouth, 27 September 2006

Myth and Mrs

The Abominable Snowman married a virgin –
All vows and rings and confetti –
But when it came to making love that night
His bride said, "Oh, no – not Yeti!"

Portsmouth, 31 December 2006

From Darda to Dum Dum

The magical flow of the East,
A-bubble below the clear skies;
To the stranger – an exotic feast
For the stomach, the heart and the eyes.

I can capture a glimpse for a moment
In this land of the Soul and the Sun,
With the feeling of joyous atonement –
With my self and the World as at one.

Madras, 25 September 1979

Keeping an Idiot in Suspense

How to keep an idiot in suspense
Without causing too much sorrow –
Well, it is actually very easy –
Hold on and I'll tell you tomorrow.

Winchester, 29 April 2006

On the Rebound

I would love you but for fault in love
For caught in love I'm sure
That all that is and ought in love
Was sought in love before –

And seeking love is losing love,
And losing love, I find,
Will only bring the birth of love
More urgently to mind.

Gosport, 28 March 1978

Past Glories

To have daughtered,
To have sonned –
The greatest purpose is to procreate the species
And the act of doing so is the greatest joy.

A young woman,
Her hair like a fountain on my face –
We worked away relentlessly
To preserve the human race.

A naked woman in my naked arms,
Our hearts and souls and bodies as at one –
Every cry,
Every touch,
Every whisper,
Every thought.

The breast was made to man a hand,
Manhood was made to play.

And the little things –
The tease,
The joke,
The sigh.

Gone now – the youthful intercourse,
The making of the product of a love –
All behind me till I die.

Sebringville, Ontario, 27 September 2007

The Perfect Host

I returned home late one evening,
My stomach notwithstanding –
I fancied something special
And it stood there on the landing.

I washed it, bashed it, cooked it
And then nibbled it on toast –
You can say what you like about me,
But I make the perfect host.

In car, 3 January 2008

41

Parting

Parting – no more is there to say! I find
No rhyme to imitate the dread. A love so blind
That it cannot see itself has no rest in words.
Yet the spasms of the gestures of my thoughts, like herds
Of unmeaning myths, pollute the contours of my tongue to
    say –
To render reasons, to shout, to rave, to betray
The inner death. And deep within the poor
Pathetic body of my soul, life's memories soar,
Through the dryness of my veins, in one final, bloody tear.
But not a sigh, not a whisper, and if there were there is no ear
To catch this fatal tone. Humanity in all her wisdom shows
No mercy to the wretched skin of a life where the broken lover
    goes.

Death is upon me, within me – love is the dying ember's
    proof.
No other words to comfort me when this alone is truth.

Bombay (Mumbai), 20 September 1979

Going with the Flow

I'm not in a hurry,
I go with the flow –
I'm coming into Surrey
And I'm late for work – but so?

Cars go flying past me –
Even the bikes are faster –
But time does not decree,
With me I am the master.

In car, 25 October 2007

I am a Quorn-Again Christian

I am a Quorn-Again Christian,
Meat is not for me.
I live out my Christian life
With this philosophy −

That we should respect all living things −
It's a fair view and it's mine −
But in Communion I have to think
That bread is bread and wine is wine.

Portsmouth, 17 September 2006

M25

Two slow-moving car parks
For clockwise trips and anti's −
Designed, it seems, to strain the heart
And saturate the panties.

In car, 2 April 2006

I Think the Bin Men found Me

I think the bin men found me,
I had crawled into the alley;
The rats were sat around me,
All curious and pally.

When you're feeling low
Please don't turn to drink −
The sad results will show
That you're lower than you think.

Portsmouth, 16 October 2007

Fellow Earthlings

Aeons ago my
Ancestors crawled –
Yours may have scurried
And mine may have roared.

But perhaps your forefathers
On my kinsfolk fed,
Thousands of yours
May have rendered mine dead.

In many lost lives
Our ancestors met,
And in many more lives
Our descendants will yet.

Through millions of years
The time has to pass,
But this life and death cycle
It seems such a farce.

Me now a human
And you now a bird –
This game we are playing
Is really absurd.

Winchester, 8 December 2005

Nothing

Nothing –
It is as simple as that –
Nothing in the bread bin,
Nothing for the cat.

Not a thing I give away,
With nothing in return –
Nought on Earth is paid to me
For nothing can I earn.

A world without a reason,
A love, a shred of care;
Nothing in the dreams we had,
Nothing everywhere.

Strange that once the concept
We both refused to see –
But nothing now in retrospect –
For you, for us, for me.

Birmingham, 30 May 1976

Bleeding Ego Islands

"Just the day for an aria!" –
Proclaims the distant sign,
And the hedgerows form a barrier
Between its world and mine.

Along a path comes struggling
The substance of my soul,
Irresistibly juggling
Its parts within its whole.

At my feet, for all to see,
My guilty conscience lies.
I see another life for me,
My guilty conscience dies.

Birmingham, 12 January 1977

Curiositydotcom

Not wishing to miss out
She joins me on my lap
And turns my current document
Into a sad mishap.

A jumble of letters on e-mail
The other day she attempted to send,
And spookily with a question mark
Stuck there on the end.

Portsmouth, 26 July 2006

On Reconciliation with God

The thinking mind alters life with each direction,
Forces pain upon itself within its quest to see.
The thinking mind is determined, unashamed;
The pulse of reason beats;
Frustration's sighs proclaim.

A bird,
Like the shadow of a radiant light upon the sky,
Drifts in triumph by –
Thoughtless,
One,
Supreme.

Here, the dreamers dream beyond;
There, the dreamer's dream.

Uxbridge, 25 January 1979

Fifty Miles to London

Come on, move your carcass,
It's time to hit the road.
You say you've had enough of this –
Oh dear! Well, I'll be blowed!

Two hundred miles to see a play –
"Rosencrantz and Guildenstern are Dead." –
You're the one who wanted to see it –
We could have stayed at home in bed.

In car, 6 October 2007

My Toilet Flushes in E flat

My toilet flushes in E flat –
I could ask for nothing finer –
And so much better than my previous one,
Which flushed in E flat minor.

Portsmouth, 22 September 2006

Brighton and Hove Actually

"My house is not in Brighton –
I'm far too good for that!"

"So, you live in Hove, then,
You pretentious little t**t!?"

Hove Actually, 7 May 2006

A Rottweiler Next Door to Me

A rottweiler next door to me –
I'm terrified of him.
His every ounce
Would love to pounce
And my chances would be slim.

I sit out in my garden
All motionless and tense
And he watches me
So silently
From behind the broken fence.

Portsmouth, 4 October 2006

Give Me Strength!

Give me strength! Give me hope!
Let not my seedlings die!
Life is babes and bathwater –
What a wasteful thing am I!

The stars above had purpose,
But then I let it slip
That I had changed and then, my friends,
My fortune took a dip.

I walk with you, hand in hand,
Along the peaceful shore –
There was a golden beach ahead,
But it is there no more.

In car, 14 January 2007

Not Going Swimmingly

As a goldfish I would drown myself
Stuck in that tank all day,
But then to end it all with gills attached
I would need some other way.

Perhaps I would tangle my neck in some reeds
And hang myself there in the drink,
But my gills would still work and I would not drop,
So I would need a subsequent think.

And a lack of hands would not help my cause,
I would have to starve or somehow take air –
For the suicidal goldfish it seems
That life would be somewhat unfair.

Hove, 30 April 2006

Who Invented the Motorcar?

Who invented the motorcar?
It's been around awhile, be assured –
Moses came down the mountain in his triumph
And the twelve disciples were in one accord.

So you ask, "Was it a divine invention?"
My response is a yes indeed 'un –
Genesis, chapter three, verse twenty-four –
"...God drove him out of the garden of Eden."

Portsmouth, 20 June 2006

CPR?

CPR? – I can't even spell it! –
And he's dead anyway! I can smell it! –
You only have to look at the flies!

A diet of burgers and hot dogs
And eventually some of the blood clogs –
So it really is no surprise.

Portsmouth, 26 May 2006

Him, Claudius

He was the greatest chicken-killer of all time –
And how, you may ask, can I tell? –
Well, Shakespeare is a reliable source,
And he says he "Did murder most foul."

Farnborough, 11 April 2006

The Way of Zen – and Men

The dying man behind the face, holding the bars
That cage his angry eyes, perceives the stars
Above. Only then, the glimmer of a hope;
Only then does the withered hand stretch and grope
For the sky. All his life the truth to seek;
Silent now, alone and weak.

And the stars flash to greet his final breath,
That a man can see such reasoning in death.

Calcutta, 3 October 1979

A Sewer can fall down a Sewer

A sewer can fall down a sewer,
But you can't teach a sow to sow;
A Polish man can polish,
But crews that row can't row.

You can subject a subject to a test;
You can shed a tear about a tear;
When I bow before my scary boss
She can see the bow in my hair.

You can present someone with a present,
But you can't teach the wind to wind –
In the English language
Things spelt the same you'll find.

Our farmers produce good produce
All across our fertile nation –
English is so hard to learn
With all this duplication.

Bordon, 31 August 2007

Between the Dreams of Time

The past is but a vision of what has seemed to be –
I cannot glimpse the purpose of its rhyme.
Through all the years of memories I have now come to see
That was has seemed was not a part of time.

The future waits upon the needs of what I seek today –
A thing to change and yet a thing assured.
To work towards a certain plan will lead one's plans astray
So thoughts of what might be must be ignored.

And here we are together between the dreams of time;
No need to think, to wait, to wonder why –
Two lights upon a meaning, so simple yet sublime,
That illuminate through each eternal now.

Gosport, 5 April 1980

Post Op

Don't worry, you'll still be able to walk –
There is no need for alarm –
The reason you're struggling to feel your leg
Is that I've amputated your arm.

Portsmouth, 25 April 2006

Room 102

I'm glad I'm not staying next door;
I hear nothing but screaming from there.
They asked if I'd move along today;
Said my room was in need of repair.

But what I want, back down in reception,
Is the key to Room 103.
If I have to go the other way
What will become of me?

Elkton, Florida, 17 September 2007

Copenhagen, 2003

Standing at the seaside –
Why is the Little Mermaid so little?
I could slap it right in the eye
With the projection of some spittle.

Life is full of disappointment,
Anticipation's better –
I'm going back to England
Where soon I should forget her.

In car, 14 January 2007

What's a Metaphor?

What's a metaphor? –
Who needs them anyway? –
But with every ounce of effort
They still won't go away.

Portsmouth, 25 September 1993

Just a Thong at Twilight

Just a thong at twilight –
That is all I like to wear –
And thus allow my special bits
To get sufficient air.

I stroll around within the house
With no friction on my sores
And I have found myself a novel way
To negotiate the doors.

Portsmouth, 15 June 2006

If the Slug had Wings

If the slug had wings
How revolting that would be,
A dollop flying in the face –
You'd want to scream and flee.

A cold and sticky lump
Of self-indulgent fat –
There'd be nothing on the windscreen –
Then one enormous splat!

They'd zoom out and attack you
As you wander by the hedge
And squadrons of the creatures
Would fly in and eat your veg.

In this diverse world of ours
We should be grateful for some things,
One of which you can't dispute –
That slugs do not have wings.

Portsmouth, 23 November 2006

Tripping over the Cat

It is my main form of exercise
And of course not much at that,
But I do it many times a day –
Tripping over the cat.

All right I am unlikely
To overcome the fat,
But at least it is something –
Tripping over the cat.

And feline immobility is
Far more hazardous than a mat,
So I will continue with the practice –
Tripping over the cat.

Portsmouth, 30 September 2006

From Droxford to Oxford

From Droxford to Oxford –
Our son has been accepted –
And in a month from now his bedroom
Will be thoroughly disinfected.

At last someone with talent
To keep the family name
And life for us in rural Hampshire
Will never be the same.

In car, 19 September 2006

After the Storm

Into each life some rain must fall
And torrential it can be;
In sunny pastures, sweet and bright,
My true love came to me.

The wind of fate upon the face
To burden me like lead;
Now, the fragrant scent of love
To breathe on us instead.

Claps of thunder through the years
To criticise and scorn;
One great triumphant final burst
On the day our love was born.

Each flash of lightning as a hope
Came and died before;
But now the radiant light of love
Is ours for evermore.

On train, 27 October 1987

I LOVE TO flout CONVENT-ION

I Love to flout convention
To upset the status quo:
it's the only Thing in life
That i enjoy, you know

All these little petty rules;
They *really* *get* *my* goat;
Give **me a pernickety person**
And I'll shake him by the throat.

PORTSMO-
UTH, October the 18th MMVI

Alone Now

Alone now
With the sunset
And with the thoughts of you.
Alone now
In the longing
And in the memory of the longing for the time
        to never end.

I sit,
A thinking stillness,
Resigned to be a stillness in your heart.

Never-ending, the night begins;
All-beginning, our love has died.

Marrakech, 21 January 1980

Regret

In the dark you brought me home last night,
And I admit I had been drinking,
But with the gift of morning light
I must ask, "What was I thinking?"

Portsmouth, 23 November 2006

Nouveau Riche

She considered herself to be posh,
Came out with "I say" and "My gosh" –
But it was really a farce –
She was of low class
And just happened to have come into dosh.

Portsmouth, 4 October 2006

Wearing Top Hat and Tails

Wearing top hat and tails
In good view from the beach,
Climbing high up in the sails –
Watch me pass, I do beseech –

Bobbing along and creating a foam –
How utterly, terribly posh –
Port out, starboard home –
Solent, Medway, Wash.

Portsmouth, 9 February 2007

The Wood for the Trees

I love you,
I love you,
All I know is true –
And all I know, my lovely,
Is of my love for you.

Things seem so different now –
My memory lacks direction
And what was once so simple
Lies confused.
Your dainty smile impaired in me distortion
The like of which no man of thought can bear –
And, unable to resist, I watched you,
Perceiving beauty in the ripest of its forms,
Until my sight had clouded my concern.

I love you,
I love you,
All I know is true –
And all I know, my lovely,
Is of my love for you.

On train, 21 September 1977

Full of Sound and Furry

Caterwauling in the garden,
My persistent little feline –
My slipper to his mouth
About to do a beeline.

Every good night's sleep
Tragically affected –
When I opted for a pet
This was not what I expected.

Winchester, 22 March 2007

The Beauty and the Clown

I offered a heart that's true,
You brought the food and wine –
All entertainment came from you
And all the blemishes were mine.

We shared the loving cup –
The Beauty and the Clown –
When you're up you're up,
But then there's only down.

In car, 4 October 2007

The Adventures of Souperman

Flask in hand he sets out for
His next eight-hour shift;
En route he buys a chocolate bar
To give himself a lift.

No one at work to chatter with,
No friends at home to see;
His family all abandoned him
In nineteen ninety-three.

Living out his boring life
At work, at home, at play –
He washes out his flask each night
For another soup next day.

Portsmouth, 23 September 2006

The Great Giuseppe Verdi

The Great Giuseppe Verdi,
All of his operas I've seen,
But I'm not the sad pretentious sort
So to me he's just Joe Green.

In car, 18 October 2006

Diary of a Salesman

Vacuum cleaners echoing
The sound of subdued thought
Gather at the doorway,
As rightly so they ought.

Mrs Sarah Sanderson,
Children both at school,
Abundantly voluptuous –
Curvy, blonde and tall.

The smell of cakes regurgitates
The appetites of lust –
Chasing her, embracing her,
As rightly so I must.

But tell it not to radios
For they can only speak –
This married mother's will is strong,
But gladly flesh is weak.

Birmingham, 23 February 1977

Without Cricket

If there is a heaven
Then cricket is its game;
Without cricket on its golden lawns
Death wouldn't be the same.

Without cricket through eternity
All would not be well –
I would have to say, regrettably,
That Heaven would be Hell.

Farnborough, 9 November 2006

It's Enough to Make You Spit

My partner hates the dentist –
Last week I took her there –
To support her at her time of need,
To show her that I care.

In the waiting room she fainted –
I managed to revive her –
But what amazed me was
Her production of saliva.

Then the dentist called her in –
I sat with her just in case –
And he used this noisy tube
To suck inside her face.

With glands like hers, I have to say,
Who needs bottled water? –
And I'm worried that she'll pass this trait
On to a son or daughter.

The dentist said she probably
Drinks three pints every day –
The romance in our relationship
In that moment went away.

He said it aids digestion,
But you'd think the Lord would find
A better way to do the job –
Something more refined.

And he added, "When you suck a sweet –
It's revolting, but it's true –
You can't avoid the fact
For all you really do –

Is flavour that saliva –
It's like downing half a glass."
So please! – No more sweets for me! –
I think I'd rather pass!

I'll have my partner's glands removed –
It might seem rather spiteful –
But in the greater scheme of things
A dry mouth sounds delightful.

Portsmouth, 27 November 2006

On a Special Species

A   A
scratch, stretch,
Then across the floor
......With n⊖t an atom out ⊖f place......
God had found perfection
When He created Cat.
That face of fur,
Sheer elegance,
An independent air.
Out by night,
Sleeping by day –
Evolution, in the cat,
Has had Her wicked way.
When you own a cat, ironically,
Well you don't, the cat owns you –
You are dominated by something
That is soft and small and cute –
Then there are the macho men
Who cannot cope with that.
God had found perfection
When He created Cat..................:

Enfield, 7 July 2007

71

Worlds Away

A sulphur field raging like a furnace,
Flowing as the flying creatures by –
And all that lives beneath its fiery surface
Ensures the fact that everything must die.

I know that somewhere worlds away you love me,
But what of love can dreamers ever claim? –
Pensive there somewhere some way above me
Where bliss and empty blackness seem the same.

Birmingham, 6 May 1977

How Green is My Alley?

How green is my alley? –
Well, there's a bin full of plastic
And bundles of paper –
It isn't fantastic –

But it's a contribution
Towards saving the planet.
So at least do as I do –
It can't hurt you now, can it?

Portsmouth, 28 September 2006

Social Insecurity

People sharing oxygen with a barren room:
Young woman crying
With baby newly born;
A man, thumping desk,
Eyes all grim and worn;
And another in conversation
With comrades of the brain –
Each question seems rhetorical,
But he answers just the same.
And the woman there,
What wrinkles tell
Only she can say –
Fumbling gloves,
Grunting groans,
Mumbling over pay.

People all alone,
People without gain –
The epitome of human kind
In an unkind air of pain.

Fareham, 31 March 1976

Envelopes are Great as Gloves

Envelopes are great as gloves –
An A5 one on each hand.
People just make fun of me,
But they don't understand –

They're cheap, and bubble-wrap inside
Makes them cosy, you should note –
And brown envelopes are special
Since they match my duffel coat.

In car, 3 September 2006

If Only I'd been Burly

If only I'd been burly
And not a little weed.
At this rate
I won't get a mate
Until I've turned to seed.

I fancy someone pretty,
But she won't notice me –
A golden bloom
Beyond my room
Is all she'll ever be.

Portsmouth, 27 November 2006

Pain

Pain can really be a pain,
It stops me having fun –
If it were not for the pain I'd feel
I'd run and run and run.

I'd enjoy cold winter mornings,
I'd not be deterred by heat,
I would allow verrucas
To flourish on my feet.

A splinter could be ignored,
Indigestion would be fine;
I'd sit in soft and easy chairs
Not bothered by my spine.

A heart attack would not phase me,
I'd not suffer with a stroke –
Without pain I'd live my life
As a contented bloke.

I'd not notice as my ailments
Slowly pass me by
And in a blissful state of ecstasy
Quite suddenly I'd die.

Havant, 9 October 2006

There was a Young Lady from Kandy

There was a young lady from Kandy
Whose boyfriend was forceful and randy.
When exhausted she said,
"You're not coming in bed,"
He replied, "On the sofa'd be dandy!"

Gosport, 28 April 1980

Playing Gooseberry

You two lovebirds holding hands
And I just follow on –
I had a love like yours once,
But now that love has gone.

Take me to the cinema,
Take me to a show –
As your bond increases
My bitterness will grow.

Portsmouth, 18 September 2006

Forever Finland

They freed one little country,
Propelled it into space –
An alien civilisation
To help the human race.

They couldn't save the rest of us,
Global warming thwarted that –
Sun cream every morning
And don't forget the hat.

So there they go, the lucky ones,
Up into the sky –
Last chance to wave the future
Of humanity goodbye.

In car, 18 July 2006

Antidisestablishmentarianism

Antidisestablishmentarianism
Is a word I like to utter –
I tend to use it frequently
So it's a good job I don't stutter.

I'm not sure what it means,
But it does sound intellectual,
And I will try most anything
To be less ineffectual.

In car, 25 October 2006

As Quiet as a Mousse

I try not to feed my partner
With anything that crunches,
I put in grapes and yoghurt
When I'm preparing her packed lunches.

No one should be subjected to
The habits she displays,
Especially with crisps she has
The loudest eating ways.

It doesn't help that her mouth
Is open when she chews –
Celery, nuts and poppadoms –
For us it's all bad news.

But in the Dessert War we have
At least achieved a truce –
It's boring, but there's nothing that's
As quiet as a mousse.

Brighton, 26 November 2006

In the Land with not a Flower

In the land with not a flower
To compliment the air
I wandered through a shower
With a fruit bat in my hair.

As lonely as an icicle
Hanging down in June,
Walking with my bicycle
Beneath a red balloon –

When suddenly I saw,
Just like a stabbing pain,
A taste I'd never heard before,
And I'll never smell again.

Gosport, 18 April 1976

Your Steaminess

I'm so sorry, Your Steaminess –
I forgot about your shower
And the fact that you stay in there
For the best part of an hour.

Some of us have work to do –
In the Rat Race I'm a rat –
But at least in time you'll waste away –
All that steam should see to that.

Brighton, 26 November 2006

Perusing the Menu

Turkey £6.25
Chicken £5.20
Each child £3.55 –
Well, one child should be plenty.

Portsmouth, 2 December 2006

Untouched by Human Hand

The passing moods of the passing crowds –
From gentle roar to piercing sigh –
The moving face afraid to stare,
Looking for a way to answer why.

A brush and then a brush aside,
A glance without reply –
A stranger gone, a stranger left –
Looking for a way to answer why.

Killarney, 7 August 1980

Moonbase 24

I perform my work with confidence
Without fear of the unknown –
It's the silence that affects me
When I'm walking out alone –

Beneath that misty orange globe
As I value what I'm worth –
With more life on this barren rock
Than there is up there on Earth.

Portsmouth, 23 August 2006

O Come all Ye Wasteful!

Half a burger for the seagulls,
Some pavlova for the flies –
We bite and then we throw away –
The Third World aches and sighs.

In car, 30 January 2007

Yet Another Ulcer!

Yet another ulcer –
That's the twenty-third this year!
I have to sit and ask myself,
"Why won't they disappear?"

I've tried that jelly stuff
And warm water with some salt –
Within reason I'd do anything
All this agony to halt.

I've used hydrogen peroxide,
But of this I am not fond –
I'm worried that, orally,
I might become a blonde.

I won't try it, but a neighbour
Said I should suck upon a leech –
And someone, not a friend of mine,
Suggesting gargling with bleach.

I suppose I will have to accept
That my poor life is fated,
That I will go on till the end
Like this – all ulcerated.

Portsmouth, 6 October 2006

We're Pink Therefore we're Ham

We may ponder what life is –
This puzzle still not cracked –
But in the end we must all die –
That is a certain fact.

In car, 4 October 2005

Provincial Thinking

The driver in front slowed down
And I hit him hard up the rear.
And when I asked, "Why didn't you indicate?" –
He replied, "But I always turn here!"

Portsmouth, 12 April 2006

Music to My Eyes

Cast the spell of purity,
The bold triumphant strain –
Show the vast assembly
That love alone must reign.

The strings draw out a melody,
Each note a precious sign –
Adoration in the gallery
For what is sheer divine.

Hail the one and only!
Praise the great unknown!
Agitate every atom
Of this building's marble stone!

An afternoon of Mozart –
So ineffable! So right!
But I know that in your virgin smile
Real pleasure comes tonight!

Birmingham, 30 November 1976

Someone Should Clean the Loo

Someone should clean the loo –
Whose name is on the rota? –
O what am I to do
With this enormous floater?

Adding more substance to it
Is simply not an option –
It's such a gigantic poo it
Could go up for adoption.

Portsmouth, 24 June 2007

Armageddonian Woe

Like Ezekiel's vision
They came in from the blue –
The year was twenty sixty-three
And my love for you was true.

When hope still had a meaning
We watched one passing by;
We followed at a distance;
We heard another's cry.

They met down by the river,
They watched the water flow –
You were always optimistic
And though I begged you not to go –

You ran down past their silver sphere
And offered them your hand –
I see you now in ghostly form
When winds disturb the sand.

"Is it right to kill your children?"
Asks a worn and broken sign.
Well, now they have my lover's life
They might as well have mine.

Gosport, 20 September 1975

Well, Fancy That!

Poetry in motion –
The rustle of her hair –
The perfect form,
Hot and warm,
Beneath her underwear.

I sigh, as a red-blooded
Male I must –
Partly out
Of awe, no doubt,
But mainly out of lust.

Waterlooville, 26 September 2006

Is there Life in Fun Town?

Is there life in Fun Town?
Will there be joy for me tonight? –
At a party or a hoedown? –
Please, can you see a light?

I'm entering phase two
Of *When-you-left-and-what-came-after*,
Still deeply missing you,
But contemplating laughter.

In car, 18 October 2007

A and Not-A

The world forever changing –
Nothing stays the same –
We need to find stability –
It's the fundamental aim.

But the Sun into the Earth,
But the Earth into a bee,
But a diamond into dust,
But my breakfast into me.

Everything in a state of flux
From birth to death and after –
Evolving, turning, moving –
Comedy, tragedy, laughter.

Sebringville, Ontario, 26 September 2007

I Think it was a Mammal

I think it was a mammal –
A dik-dik or a deer,
An onyx or a great elk, perhaps,
Or maybe a tapir.

It rushed out from the roadside
And jumped in front of me –
Skilfully I avoided it
And crashed into this tree.

It might have been an elephant
Or bigger still – I think.
But I do assure you, officer,
I have not had a drink.

In car, 6 October 2006

The Problem with Bananas

The problem with bananas
Is that they're much too yellow;
The problem with my postman
Is that he's a boring fellow.

The problem with a harbinger
Is that it speaks of doom;
The problem with my thoughts
Is that they plague me room to room.

The problem with a parody
Is in what it fails to say,
And that applies when I get down
Upon my knees and pray.

The problem with my parrot
Is that she can't be free –
I see problems everywhere
Since you walked out on me.

Portsmouth, 14 September 2006

Shakespeare is so Wonderful

"A horse, a horse," "*Et tu, Brute*,"
"To be or not to be?" –
Shakespeare is so wonderful,
It means so much to me.

From "the quality of mercy"
To "a plague on both your houses!" –
The excitement it encourages,
The spirit it arouses.

Through "fair and foul" and "dusty death"
One thing I guarantee:
That Shakespeare will go on and on
Throughout eternity.

Havant, 14 September 2006

On the Edge of Shadow

On the edge of shadow
I stood beside a tree
And a little fluffy robin
Hopped along to me.

We chatted for some time,
But when I had to go
I turned to glance behind me
And he was there, you know –

Eagerly pursuing me,
My attention still to seek –
Life is full of meaning
When nature is so meek.

Portsmouth, 3 February 2008

Goodbye Mr. Richardson

Goodbye Mr. Richardson –
Your wife was for the taking
And I was among all others
That she should have been forsaking –

Seductive and voluptuous
With deep hypnotic eyes –
I weakened through her kisses,
I melted to her sighs.

Goodbye Mr. Richardson –
Although we never met
Leaving you with your wife
Was the best gift you could get.

Portsmouth, 29 December 2007

One Dead Leaf

One dead leaf
To represent the World:
The slither of the snake,
The trampling tyrannosaur,
The monkey, the hydra,
King Philip the Second of Spain –
Sunlight, nutrients, life –
No leaf has died in vain.

Portsmouth, 5 September 2007

A Christmas Kiss

A Christmas kiss
From Elizabeth –
I hold my breath
And sigh –
Her lips so hot,
To leave them not
I can but only try.

Gosport, 21 December 1976

My New Hawaiian Shirt

My new Hawaiian shirt –
Some people say it's sad.
At least you can see me in a crowd,
But you might not wish you had.

Gosport, 19 August 2006

Through the Lens of Time

With me through each moment, then –
Now a photo in my drawer.
So, why did I leave you when
I could have never wanted more?

Sitting here and asking why –
What happened to me there? –
Did I ever really try?
Did I ever care?

I look upon your restful eyes,
Burning now to know –
And every ounce of being tries
To cry, "I need you so!"

The camera cannot lie, they say,
So when I left you then
Why was there not the urge to stay
And look at you again?

How wretched is the irony –
To see your smile appear –
All those years away from me,
Yet, for the first time – here!

Gosport, 19 October 1980

Each Face

Each face is a lonely face –
A desert, where despair
Pollutes the oasis of the mind.

Each smile is a lonely smile –
A brick upon the wall of grief,
An irony of pain.

We hide, but from ourselves –
We are the cold –
We miss the meanings and live the lies.

Calcutta, 4 October 1979

Step into the World

Step into the world.
Your room is lonely now;
Your soul in need of comfort.

Step into the world.
The darkness is within you;
Out there the hope prevails.

Step into the world.
Be there mist or fog or haze
The future lies beyond.

Step into the world.
Be bold and make the effort –
Your moment has arrived.

Portsmouth, 29 January 2007

The Search

I exist and God exists –
His time permits my stay –
He is Truth, so I am told –
And we from Truth must stray.

In this world of ignorance,
Our sad domain of doubt –
God is sought within, they say –
So why this search without?

San Francisco, California, 1 July 1973

Buses

Buses brought me to you,
Buses saw us part –
I blame it all on buses
For buses broke my heart.

In my room and lonely,
As now I tend to be,
I watch the passing buses
And think of you and me.

They have their destinations,
Must see their journeys through –
I just sit and watch them
With no route back to you.

Birmingham, 1 December 1975

Lettuce with a Gladsome Mind

Lettuce with a gladsome mind
Grew on Earth to mock mankind –
We are tragic things, my dear –
We mourn before our roots appear.

Cabbage with a joyful heart
Left its rivals at the start –
We are morbid things, you know –
We abandon life before we grow.

Gosport, 22 August 1975

A Busty Young Girl Called Louise

A busty young girl called Louise
Said to the barman, just for fun –
"I'll have a *double entendre*, please!" –
And to oblige, he gave her one.

Portsmouth, 29 August 2007

What is it with Sucky Sweets?

What is it with sucky sweets? –
I cannot resist a bite.
If I sucked it through to its end
There is every chance I might –

Get ten more minutes of pleasure
And thus less of life's great pain.
But, no! Oh, dear! Here I go! –
I have bitten it again!

In car, 12 September 2006

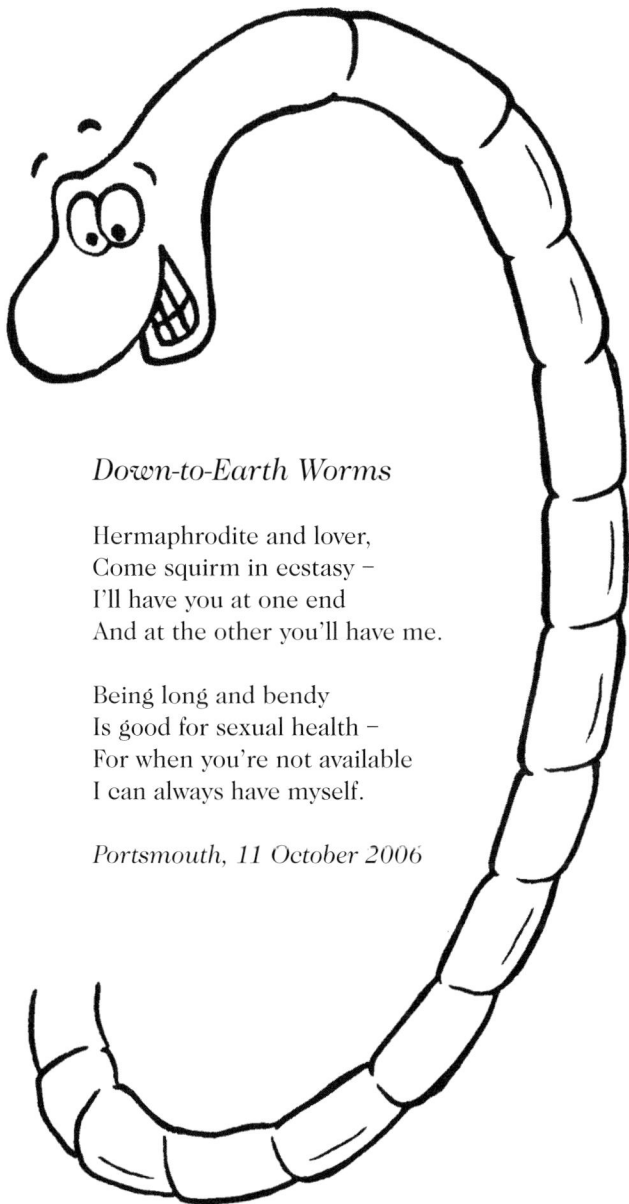

Down-to-Earth Worms

Hermaphrodite and lover,
Come squirm in ecstasy –
I'll have you at one end
And at the other you'll have me.

Being long and bendy
Is good for sexual health –
For when you're not available
I can always have myself.

Portsmouth, 11 October 2006

Thoughts on a Bike

The need to find another way
Of broadening the mind
Has found me here with Kate before
And Angela behind.

The aim in life, one fancies,
Could be in the way one feels –
Seeking out a public bar
Upon a pair of wheels.

But far be it that I should sit
And leave the rest to fate –
Wobbling here uneasily
'Tween Angela and Kate.

I'm happy, but I have to say
That this is hardly funny –
Working here without work,
Without pride and without money.

Then rolling on unceasingly
I hear the sudden cry –
"If we don't get there soon enough
I swear I'm gonna die!"

Well, this could be the meaning
Of the vision I'm now seeing –
Living life to the full
Could be the purpose of our being.

But still I have to wonder
If our endeavour here is right,
Wheeling off so penniless
Upon the verge of night –

And true that with the social arts
No gentleman should meddle –
But damn what's fair! – Come on you pair! –
We're nearly there! – So peddle!

Gosport, 26 August 1980

'Ere!!

She's coming back again –
She fills my heart with fear –
When she needs to make a point
She starts it off with "'Ere!!"

Her voice, all shrill and piercing,
Has a quality so rare,
And whenever she is talking
I wish I were "elsewhere."

Winchester, 29 August 2006

Mistaken Identity

Hedgehogs have fingerprints similar to ours
And for that I should give praise –
I robbed a bank the other day
And they arrested a hedgehog in Hayes.

Portsmouth, 22 September 2006

We were Lovers

We were lovers
In the truest sense of the word –
"Were," that is –
Or at least, I was.

Birmingham, 12 January 1978

Fast Food

Hot dogs are jet propelled,
Burgers zoom for miles,
Spicy chicken wings leave their rivals
Standing in the aisles.

And they reckon that a pizza slice
Can run a nifty race.
As for me, eating all this junk
I wouldn't last the pace.

Portsmouth, 25 September 2006

Sortie Imminent

I grew tired of my sat nav –
The same old English voice –
I considered other options
And "French Female" was my choice.

I find it very sexy
When she tells me where to go –
I take directions from her
Even when I know.

I must admit I struggle
With the language problem, but
At least I know the difference now
Between my *gauche* and *droite*.

In car, 26 October 2006

In the Autumn

In the Autumn
I watch the new life grow –
The buds of power,
The leaves of joy.
Hope springs maternal –
A lamb to run,
A chick to cry.

By being,
Through adventure,
In wonder,
With love.

In the Autumn
I see the meaning,
But it is far too late for me.

In car, 3 November 2007

All of a Heap

I could fill a thousand hippo bags
With all the stuff in here,
But can I dispose of it? –
No, none of it, I fear.

I am just a hoarder,
Every item has a past –
The sentimental value
Of everything is vast.

Day by day I watch the piles
As they accumulate –
With a crush or suffocation
Awaiting as my fate.

Portsmouth, 1 December 2006

I've Never Seen a Cat Faint

I've never seen a cat faint,
But I suppose a meerkat might –
It happens when your head is high,
When you spend your time upright.

And fate has intervened –
It was destined to affect us –
It comes with the territory
When you're *homo erectus*.

In car, 13 August 2007

On a Step Too Far

In the choir these days it is not easy to find
A song that is PC to sing.
So perhaps they should play a concerto instead –
By Schuperson or Mendeloffspring.

Portsmouth, 9 September 2006

My Dreams of Her

I only have my dreams of her,
My stupid adoration.
I cannot alter divine plan,
Cannot make her feel for me,
Cannot bring down God to sow the wretched earth –
Only when you've loved without an answer
Can you know what nothingness is worth.

Nottingham, 5 November 1977

Like Father, Like Son

Dear worms, our task is done here –
There's nothing left but hunger.
But fear not and be of good cheer
For we've still got Pitt the Younger.

Portsmouth, 10 November 2007

The Mourning After

Thinking of the silky down of pleasure,
Leaving you as if you never cared –
What was it to our love in leisure
That my request so tragically impaired?

To touch your breasts, to give you what was needed,
To squeeze out from your nakedness all hope –
I waited for the moment and pleaded,
But all I got, pure vanity, was, "Nope!"

On train, 8 July 1977

On the Fab One

Listening to the Pope conducting mass
Sung flat in some dreadful lingo –
I'm sure Pope John Paul had a better voice –
So let's hope next for a Pope George Ringo.

Portsmouth, 16 September 2006

Turn of Events

One annoying fact,
It causes me to frown –
Women and the toilet seat –
Why do they leave it down?

Steep, 1 February 2007

My Cereal Collection

I've been sticking them in books
Since nineteen sixty-three –
One specimen per packet –
Would you like to come and see?

I've got fifty volumes –
Ten on every shelf –
And every single packet
I have consumed myself.

Persisting with a hobby
Is a very healthy sign –
Have what you like for breakfast,
But the cereal is mine.

Enfield, 20 January 2007

Loving You Platonically

Loving you platonically
As days and weeks drift by –
In this world of seems
And sordid dreams
What more could satisfy?
To share a love as we do
Is a wonder to the world –
Island beaches overlap,
Intellectually fulfil –
Smiles and graces
From caring faces
Shining in the Sun –
A hope indeed for anyone
In need to conquer sin –
Loving you platonically
And yet so sad within.

Birmingham, 14 January 1976

Time Prevails

Time prevails, and there is often
Little opportunity to wait –
As things stand I might simply
Resign myself to fate.

I get pushed hither and thither
In higgledy-piggledy ways –
Sometimes there is fun in life,
But on very special days.

I carry on as a slave –
I just dream of being the master –
On the rocky road to death –
Faster and faster and faster.

Lake Buena Vista, Florida, 20 September 2007

Archimedes' Principle

Archimedes' Principle –
I fell into the bath –
I slipped upon a bar of soap –
It made my partner laugh.

I didn't shout "*Eureka!*" –
Not with a busted lip –
But with all the water I displaced
You could have sunk a ship.

Portsmouth, 9 October 2006

Looking

Looking out
I looked upon myself
Looking for you –
But the different views confused me
And since your eyes refused me
I took to other aims,
Looked for delusion –
The easier task,
No doubt –
For looking in upon myself
I saw it looking out.

Birmingham, 9 February 1978

To a Lost Cousin

In the war you fell
Offering resistance,
But my father never knew,
Had no hint of your existence.

My father fought nearby,
He was captured, he was taken –
But you gave everything,
Your essence was forsaken.

Brave until the end
And to your country loyal,
Buried then far off
Beneath Italian soil.

For Claude Harry Wickham 1921 – 1944,
buried at the Arezzo War Cemetery, Italy.

In car, 7 February 2008

All Nonsense

Beneath the moon's marmorial snout
I live my life in vain,
Working on from day to day
With a few weeks off in Spain.

Of shoes – and ships – and sealing-wax –
I can tell you anything –
I still have my old school books
And my ex-wife's wedding ring.

To the echoing sound of a coppery gong
My world just slips away –
Another thousand sighs to wait
Until another day.

Winchester, 24 May 2006

The Passing of the Pain

The world has not succeeded in its purpose
Through this or any other tragic ploy –
The missing of the moments unceasing,
The endless fall behind the mask of joy.

We dare not watch the atmosphere engulf us,
As winter comes so too our hearts decay –
Silently we feel our lives defeat us,
No wherewithal to seek another way.

And the act is gone, forgotten,
Only threads remain:
The holding of your hand, the waiting,
The pleasure in the passing of the pain.

Uxbridge, 30 September 1978

Perhaps I should do Hieroglyphics

Perhaps I should do hieroglyphics
Or try German or Latin or Greek.
My output has become quite prolific,
But it's other styles of expression I seek.

English, of course, has its uses –
To the masses it means I am pandering,
But I can no longer make up excuses –
I should be writing this poem in Mandarin.

In car, 17 October 2007

A Gentle Tree

A gentle tree creating shade,
Basking in the light,
Magnificent through the burning day
And mysterious by night –
Firm in its foundation,
Triumphant in its height.

We are fellow creatures,
Our time on Earth to share,
But your needs are soft and secret,
You have nothing to declare –
A thousand leafy branches
Swaying in the air.

Waterlooville, 31 October 2006

Ovine, was Mine

My ex-partner was like a sheep –
He followed me around,
Agreeing to decisions
With his awful bleating sound.

I ended it the other day –
He took it very hard –
He walked into the corner,
He stood there and he baaed.

Portsmouth, 28 September 2006

Talking to Women

When I see a thing of beauty I speak, I have to do it –
When you have to do what you have to do, of course,
            you have to do it.

As a baby, mouth to nipple, I would have opted then to glue it –
I couldn't speak and it was a time when I didn't need to do it.

As a child I loved my toys, I told them so, they knew it –
We played on the floor all day long – there was the time to do it.

As a youth, unsatisfied, with my desire to pursue it –
A female form in front of me and I simply had to do it.

Through passing years there was love, but there was
            nothing to it –
Then from dusk to dusk and dawn to dawn I didn't get to do it.

The wrinkles formed, but I love youth and I'm still
            attracted to it –
To chat up blondes, brunettes, redheads – I'm afraid
            I have to do it.

Dear John, you blab, you waffle, putting your
            sad self through it –
You should cut out your tongue and walk away –
            that's the way to do it.

Portsmouth, 7 February 2008

I Love the Smell of a Curry

I love the smell of a curry,
I could sniff it from morning to night,
It's my drug and I make no excuses –
It works for me and it's right.

I love the effect that it has
And the joy as it makes my face warmer.
Next time you come round and see me
You might find me deep in a korma.

Portsmouth, 7 January 2007

Romp and Circumstance

The evidence is plain to see,
Don't keep it under cover –
That sighing did not come from me –
You've got yourself a lover!

Portsmouth, 28 August 2007

How Unpleasant as a Pheasant

How unpleasant as a pheasant
Now that traffic's here –
The joy of life, the beauty,
Then wham! – to disappear!

Portsmouth, 23 February 1999

When Two People Meet

When two people meet
The urge for them to stay
Is governed by their solitude of mind –
So the loveless say.

There is no joy in finding,
All meetings are the same,
Words and gestures are all empty –
That is the loveless claim.

But on this bright and brilliant day
Observers must agree
That in view of our togetherness
The loveless cannot see.

Gosport, 16 July 1978

All Infected Down from London

All infected down from London,
Frozen hearts and frosted eyes;
Every one a world of sorrow
In a carriage full of lies.

Passengers all participating
In the isolation game;
Never once communication;
Lost behind the guilt and shame.

What I would give to end this journey,
The struggle and will to live;
But then, in truth, what isolation
When there is nothing left to give.

Southampton, 7 April 1976

The Mug upon the Mantelpiece

The mug upon the mantelpiece –
I put it there in June.
Since then I have been saying
That I will remove it soon.

And I will do, believe me,
But it's now been there so long
That without it the whole essence
Of the décor would be wrong.

It's got a crack upon it,
I hope it doesn't leak,
There's something growing in it –
It winked at me last week.

In car, 1 December 2006

Must You Dribble on the Pillowcase?

Must you dribble on the pillowcase?
What a way to start the day –
On the spot where you have been,
All cold and damp and grey.

And it soaks through to the pillow
And leaves a yellow stain –
When I agreed to marry you
I must have been insane!

Portsmouth, 1 September 2006

Hip, Hip, Roget!

There are people who would do
All sorts of good things for us,
But my heart goes out to Roget
And his magnificent thesaurus.

It's compendious, substantial,
Consolidated and concise;
It's excellent and flawless,
Superlative and nice.

It helps us with our poetry,
It helps us with our prose –
When there are words we cannot think of
Roget's Thesaurus knows.

It enables us to elucidate,
To be explicit and discerning;
It really is a useful thing –
It facilitates our learning.

And a final note on the subject –
There's no way that you could doubt it –
We would have, without this splendid book,
Fewer things to say about it.

Winchester, 18 October 2006

I Dropped My Sock in the Lav

I dropped my sock in the lav,
I wanted to retrieve it –
But since I hadn't pulled the chain
I thought it best to leave it.

Portsmouth, 28 December 2006

I've got Writer's Block!

I've been here for ages now
Staring at the clock.
I knew it would come eventually –
I've got Writer's Block!

My wasted life is passing by
With every tick and tock.
Fate has been so cruel to me –
I've got Writer's Block!

I'd rather have pneumonia
Or some problem with my cock.
Nothing could be worse than this –
I've got Writer's Block!

There's someone at the door,
There it goes again – Knock! Knock!
I'm sorry, I can't come out and play –
I've got Writer's Block!

Portsmouth, 2 December 2006

Final Gesture

The sea moves in a melancholy way towards the epitome of
          human benevolence.
Through sustained and violent motion the subject of my fear
        shows thoughtfulness –
                What then the ending?
                What now the theme?
So let us play as infants to the coral reef –
So let us live
              and squander.
The patterns are there to be seen –
The lamps of hope
              and squander.
If we try just once more –
If we forget the quarrels –
If we make like lovers ought and drift away endlessly –
The two of us alone at the very edge of the Universe –
The two of us alone –
The two of us...

...in silence now;
My thoughts are all my own again.
I kiss your breasts.
Wet and warm we snuggle.
Soon it will be the day –
I will dress,
Gather what there is of mine
And leave your arms forever.

Gosport, 13 September 1976

Famous Last Words

"So little time, so much to do,"
Said Elizabeth the First –
Quite a clever comment
For her final little burst.

"Either that wallpaper goes or I do,"
Said Wilde, and the décor stayed –
But his death might have passed unnoticed
If he had simply prayed.

"Bugger Bognor," as he lay dying
George the Fifth was said to say,
But Bognor had the last laugh
Once he had passed away.

"Kiss me Hardy" or "*kismet*" maybe
Said Nelson ere he went –
It's good to leave controversy
When your time on Earth is spent.

"Everything has gone wrong, my girl,"
Arnold Bennett said,
And with some degree of accuracy
Since straight after he was dead.

With all this competition
Can I hope to be on par? –
I think not, and most probably
I'll just go with "Ahhh!!"

Portsmouth, 22 October 2006

Index of First Lines